Flush in the Pan

To Pad.
Keep on 'flushing'
Dulcie Lewis

Dulie Lew

COUNTRYSIDE BOOKS
NEWBURY BERKSHIRE

First published 2003
©Dulcie Lewis 2003
Reprinted 2008

COUNTRYSIDE BOOKS
3 Catherine Road
Newbury, Berkshire

To view our complete range of books,
please visit us at
www.countrysidebooks.co.uk

ISBN 978 1 85306 817 1

Printed by Information Press, Oxford

Contents

The first movement

I have few claims to fame except that for many years I have given talks on the lavatory. Discovering my interest in the history of the bath and lavatory has led people to share with me their one and only related joke or merry quip. I have always been happy to be the recipient of much loved stories and thank those fellow enthusiasts. Over the years I have assembled a classic collection of stories and one-liners that are part of the collective folk memory for those of a certain age. It is impossible to know who first told them or if they are true.

No one mourns the passing of the outdoor lavatory but with its demise we have lost something. The sense of adventure in a trip down the garden path is missing from our lives. Those born after 1950 have been deprived of the character building delights of shit shovelling. Where are the stories now of old ladies backing into an outdoor privy in the dark and finding themselves seated on a tramp's lap?

There are no tales attached to modern bathrooms except of the crudest sort. You will not find those within these pages. The old privies and WCs gave rise to witty tales perhaps reflecting universal constipation and the length of time spent sitting there.

Here then is a small book I hope anyone would be happy to have in their bathroom. May you always be blessed with a warm seat and a strong flush.

Dulcie Lewis

Down the garden path

I must down to the privy again,
To the lonely loo and the sky,
And all I ask is a warm seat
And some paper to wipe me dry,
And the cobwebs cling and the draughts sing –
And the old door creaking,
And a wet patch on my bald head
As the roof above is leaking.

(Apologies to John Masefield)

Young Willie's family had a well-built wooden garden privy situated some distance from the house, which backed onto the canal. Willie and some friends out making mischief thought it would be fun to push the privy into the canal.

Later trying to find out who had done this dark deed Willie's father questioned his son as to what part he might have played in all this. Naturally the son denied all knowledge.

Father looked saddened and told him how wrong it was to tell a lie but again Willie denied it. So father told Willie the story of George Washington, the first President of the

A Flush in the Pan

United States of America, who as a boy had secretly chopped down a cherry tree. When George Washington's father tackled his son about the tree felling the future president owned up, for he could not tell a lie, and his father forgave him and there was no punishment.

Young Willie listened thoughtfully and decided that he too would tell the truth. 'Yes Dad, it was me who pushed the privy into the canal.'

With that father took off his leather belt and gave him a sound beating. 'Owww,' cried young Willie, 'that's not fair, you said George Washington didn't get punished when he owned up!'

'Ah yes,' said father, 'but George Washington's father wasn't sitting in the tree at the time.'

Two ladies standing at a bus stop. One says to the other, 'I hear Mrs Jones is not keeping at all well at the moment'.

'Oh, what's the matter with her?'

'Chronic constipation, I'm afraid. I've known her be down her privy for over an hour!'

Says the second lady, 'I'm sorry to hear that. Is she taking anything for it at the moment?'

'Well just lately she's been taking her knitting.'

'I know it's not natural but at least it stops him hurling half bricks at us.'

A Flush in the Pan

An oil company had drilled for several months to find oil on an island off the west coast of Scotland. Eventually it was decided that there was no oil but before leaving they filled in the holes they had drilled, which were many hundreds of feet deep.

The old couple on whose land they had been drilling asked the company to leave one of the deep holes unfilled. Over this they constructed a new privy and were absolutely delighted with the arrangement for it meant that never again would they have to do any emptying.

Their son, who was an infrequent visitor, came to stay and on his first night went out to use the new privy. He was gone a long time and the old couple became worried. Father got a storm lantern and set off to look for his son.

On reaching the privy he found the lad slumped on the floor in a deep faint. Slapping his face to bring him round, he asked what had happened but all the son could say was, 'I just blacked out'.

After their son had left, the old couple sat by the fire wondering what had made him pass out. Then his mother remembered, 'Do ye no mind how young Sandy allus held his breath when he was a wee bairn ... until he heard the splash!'

If in this place you find no paper,

Behind the door you'll find a scraper.

The Country Seat

An elderly man lived in an ancient cottage deep in the countryside. A young city couple out for a walk had lost their way and stopped to ask him directions. He seemed kindly and helpful so the young woman asked if she could use his lavatory.

'Certainly,' replied the old man. 'Just go straight down the garden path.'

The young woman disappeared down the overgrown garden only to reappear seconds later very hot and bothered.

'But there's no lock on the door,' she protested.

'Don't you worry about that, my dear,' said the old man, 'there's no need for locks on our privy. I've lived here nigh on 50 years and never had a bucket of shit pinched yet.'

One lady while visiting a new acquaintance remarked: 'Your husband must be a very keen gardener, that's the third time he's said he's going out to shake the dew off the lily.'

A Flush in the Pan

Tom, Harry and 'Orsemuck had been out drinking with the lads. A few beers followed by a long walk home was too much for them, so Tom, who lived nearest the pub, invited them to sleep it off in his front room.

During the night Harry needed to 'go' and grabbing a torch from the kitchen table he made his way unsteadily down the garden path to Tom's privy.

'This torch is handy,' thought Harry, putting it down beside him. He was soon back indoors in the warm, fast asleep. Later on 'Orsemuck had a pressing need to 'go' as well. Staggering down the garden path, he could see a faint glow from under the privy door.

'That's kind of old Tom to leave a light on in there,' thought 'Orsemuck. Inside a beautiful white light shone upward, illuminating the ceiling.

'Well,' thought 'Orsemuck, settling down on the seat, 'old Tom must be doing well for 'isself – I ain't got 'lectric in my lav.'

The next morning the three pals were nursing their hangovers when 'Orsemuck said, 'Ere, I ain't seen one of those fancy privy lights afore – must've set you back a bit.'

'What light?' said Tom. 'There ain't no light in my privy 'cept a bit of moonlight.'

Then it dawned on Harry. 'Here, you know that new torch of yourn ... You could've told me you'd got a two-holer!'

'Don't worry about the flies – just hang on 5 minutes and the missus will be serving up dinner. They'll all be off down the kitchen then.'

A Flush in the Pan

❍◦❍◦❍◦❍◦❍◦❍◦❍◦❍◦❍◦❍◦❍◦❍◦❍◦❍◦❍◦❍

*A*n old couple were having a drink in a country pub. The old man had two wooden legs and found it difficult to get about, but he needed the lavatory and set off down the pub path to the outside privy. He was gone a long time and his wife became increasingly worried so she set off to look for him. As she neared the privy she heard cries for help and wrenching open the door there was the old man stuck down the privy hole with his wooden legs up in the air.

The old man was jammed fast and pull as she might there was nothing the old lady could do. Suddenly out of the corner of her eye she saw a young man nearby and pleaded with him for help. 'Can you give us a hand here, my husband is stuck down the privy.'

'He can't be,' said the young man, 'I've just been over and shut the door as some ruddy fool had left a bloomin' wheelbarrow in there.'

> If you sprinkle when you tinkle,
>
> Please be neat and wipe the seat.

❍◦❍◦❍◦❍◦❍◦❍◦❍◦❍◦❍◦❍◦❍◦❍◦❍◦❍◦❍◦❍

A Flush in the Pan

A city type out walking in the countryside got completely lost. Needing directions he saw through the undergrowth a small building and, fighting his way through. knocked loudly on the door.

The door opened slightly and a small boy peered out.

'Excuse me, is your father in?' enquired the walker.

'No,' said the young boy, *'he went out when Mam came in.'*

'Well, can I speak to your Mother then?' asked the walker.

'No,' said the young boy, *'she went out when my big sister came in.'*

'Well then, can I speak to your sister?' said the walker.

'Fraid not, she went out when I came in.'

'Listen, sonny,' said the walker, beginning to lose his patience, 'I've had enough of this, just what is this place – a mad house?'

'No, sir,' said the lad, *'it's the shit house – the house is up the other end of the garden.'*

What's in a name?

Thomas Crapper (1836-1910). The nation's plumbing safe in this man's hands. (By kind permission of Thomas Crapper & Co Ltd, Stratford-upon-Avon).

Thomas Crapper was born into a humble family in Thorne near Doncaster, leaving home at the age of 11 to walk to London. After serving his apprenticeship with a Master Plumber in Chelsea and working as a journeyman he set up in his own right in 1861. His Marlborough Works in Chelsea had a reputation for quality and service together with a distinguished telegram address – Crapper Chelsea.

He was proud to call himself a Sanitary Engineer with many patents to his name for his pioneering work on the lavatory cistern, drains and adequate ventilation. It is popularly thought that Mr Crapper invented the WC and that the vulgar word for faeces is taken from his name. Not so.

crapula	–	Latin intoxication, hangover.
crappen	–	Dutch (1100-1500) to break off.
crappe	–	English (1151-1500) a husk of grain or chaff, residue from rendered fat, dregs of beer.
crap	–	English slang 1846 to defecate.
Crapper	–	Thomas Crapper (1836-1910) Yorkshireman and pioneer plumber.
crapper	–	American troops (1914-18 War) slang name for lavatory, WC.

There once was a plumber called Crapper,

Who had an idea in his napper,

For gentry to choose

His Victorian loos,

So his bank account soon became dapper.

Don Love

A Flush in the Pan

Thomas Crapper developed and perfected the WC, in particular working long and hard on the strength of his flush. Previous high level WCs wasted large amounts of water as the valve at the outlet to the flush pipe never maintained a proper seal, and water flowed constantly. The problem was solved with Crapper's Valveless Water Waste Preventer: 'One Moveable Part – Flush with Easy Pull'.

He invented the bathroom showroom and displayed his wares in large plate glass windows. This caused quite a stir, with certain ladies becoming faint when observing the shocking sight of the china bowls.

By the 1880s Crapper & Co's reputation was such among the nobility and gentry that they were invited to supply the Prince of Wales (later Edward VII) at Sandringham. In the following years, Buckingham Palace, Windsor Castle and Westminster Abbey all benefited from Crapper's goods and services. George V continued the Royal Appointment. Plumbing and drains were very much a family interest, with King Edward's father, Prince Albert, having been much concerned with the drains at Windsor Castle – indeed many said they killed him.

Thomas Crapper died in 1910. His inventiveness and skill sounded the death knell for the outside privy, for which millions gave him thanks. A man of vision *par excellence* and a prince amongst plumbers.

The company he had founded continued, albeit without a Crapper at the helm. The business was sold in the 1960s and subsequently suffered some fallow years, but the distinguished firm of Thomas Crapper & Co has survived and is once again an independent company.

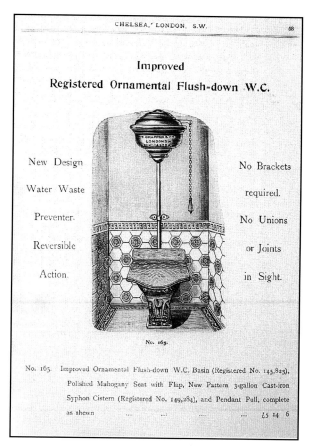

Improved
Registered Ornamental Flush-down W.C.

New Design

Water Waste

Preventer.

Reversible

Action.

No Brackets

required.

No Unions

or Joints

in Sight.

No. 165.

No. 165. Improved Ornamental Flush-down W.C. Basin (Registered No. 145,823), Polished Mahogany Seat with Flap, New Pattern 3-gallon Cast-iron Syphon Cistern (Registered No. 149,284), and Pendant Pull, complete as shewn £5 14 6

Seated on the throne. Originally made for Sandringham, then offered in an 1899 catalogue to the general public. (By kind permission of Thomas Crapper & Co Ltd, Stratford-upon-Avon).

The march of progress

An elderly couple had a brick-built bucket privy at the bottom of the yard of their little terraced house. Their soldier son was used to more modern flush facilities in the barracks and when he came home on leave he nagged his parents to modernise and install a high level, cast iron flush WC out in the yard.

Father was adamant, 'No, that bucket privy has been good enough for your mother and me and it's good enough for you.'

The argument raged on and on until finally the soldier son's patience ran out and he said, 'I'm giving you one last chance. Are you getting rid of that bucket privy?'

'No,' said father.

''Right,' said the son, reaching into his pocket and bringing out a hand grenade. Whereupon he pulled the pin and lobbed the hand grenade at the privy.

There was a huge explosion. It was a terrible scene of devastation; the privy was flattened, with bricks, slates and wood all in a smouldering heap.

Father said to the son in horror, 'What have you done? Mother was in there!' With that, father rushed down the yard shouting, 'Myrtle, Myrtle are you all right?'

Out of the dust and the dirt and the debris came a little quavery voice, 'Yes George, I think I am. It must have been something I ate!'

How can you tell you're on an Irish aeroplane?

It's got an outside lavvy.

A Flush in the Pan

Sean T. O'Kelly, an Irish politician who became President of Ireland from 1945 to 1959, had concerned himself greatly with a slum area in Dublin where there were still old bucket privies in the backyards. His great achievement as a politician was to have drainage and water installed and the privies converted into flush WCs complete with a free cleaning brush.

On completion of one project he made a visit to inspect the new lavatories and, as he was being shown round, he paused to look at one of the new water closets more closely. As he did so an old woman shot out of the adjoining lavatory brandishing a lavatory brush in the air shouting, 'Sean T. O'Kelly or no Sean T. O'Kelly, I'm going back to paper!'

A Flush in the Pan

Depends which side of the door you are on.

A German on holiday in England for the first time went into a café and after his meal needed the lavatory. Not seeing any signs and knowing the English have many different words for the lavatory he was not sure how to ask for it. Heinz called the waitress over and said, 'Excuse me miss, do you have a cloakroom?' 'No,' she replied, 'but you can use the hatstand.'

A Flush in the Pan

A farmer went to see his accountant and was told that it had been a good year for the farm and there was some spare money. The accountant encouraged the farmer to spend some of his profits.

The farmer returned home to his wife and told her the good news. 'What would you like to spend the money on, my dear?' said the old farmer.

'Do you know what I would like more than anything,' said the farmer's wife, 'I'm sick and tired of that old outside privy. I'd like to get rid of it and have a lovely new flush lavatory installed in the house.'

And the farmer agreed.

The following year the farmer visited his accountant again and was told that as in the previous year he had made plenty of money and that he should spend some of it.

The old farmer asked his wife what she would like to spend the money on this time. She thought a bit and replied, 'I've always fancied doing up the garden a bit and having a lovely patio with a barbecue.'

And the farmer agreed.

That summer the old farmer and his wife were sitting out on the new patio watching the meat cooking on their barbecue. 'You know,' he said, 'the world's a different place these days. I'm not sure I can keep up with all this progress. To think it was not that long ago we went outside to the lavatory and inside to eat and now it's completely the other way round – we eat outside and go inside to the lavvy.'

Let's hope this attracts a better class of customer.'

What do you call a woman with two lavatories? – Lulu.

What is an ig? – An eskimo's house without a loo.

Where does a bison go to the lavatory? – In a buffaloo.

○━○━○━○━○━○━○━○━○━○━○━○━○━○━○━○━○━○━○━○

Loo-phemisms

Answering the 'call of nature':

I'm going

for a Jimmy Riddle

for a slash

for a sweet pea

for a tom tit

to buy peppermints
(when in the cinema)

to change my library book

to check the moorings

to do something you
can't do for me

to freshen up

to inspect the geography
of the house

to inspect the plumbing

to make a deposit at the
bank

to pick a daisy

to pluck a rose

to point Percy at the
porcelain

to powder my nose

to see a man about a dog

to see uncle/aunty

to shake hands with an
old friend

to shake my lettuce

to shut up the hens

to spend a penny

to stack the tools

to strain the potatoes

to telephone Hitler

to the George

to the groves

to the house where the
emperor goes on foot

to the used beer
department

to turn my bicycle around

to wash my hands

to water the family tree

to water the garden

to water the horses

to wring my socks out

down the garden

out the back

up Lavender Creek

where the wind is always
blowing

○━○━○━○━○━○━○━○━○━○━○━○━○━○━○━○━○━○━○

The British Army when out in Suez had a contraption called a Desert Rose. This was a length of half-inch tubing with a metal funnel welded round the top. The tubing was sunk into the ground to a depth of 3 feet allowing everything to soak away.

The RAF had a similar funnel and tube arrangement but called a Desert Lily.

English language is rich in the alternative names for the old outdoor privy:

Aunt Jane's
Backhouse
Biffy
Bog
Boghouse
Bombay
Bucket and chuck it
Chamber of Commerce
Chuggie
Closet
Cludgie
Comfort station
Crapper box
Crapphouse
Dike
Dinkem-dunnies
Dispensary
Dover House
Dubby
Dubs
Duffs
Dunnakin
Dunny
Garderobe
Gong house
Grots
Halting station
Heads
Holy of holies
Home of rest

A Flush in the Pan

House of Commons
Houses of Parliament
Jakes
Jericho
John
Karzi
Klondike
Knickies
Larties
Latrine
Lats
Little house
Long drop
Loo
Midden
Mixen
Necessarium
Nessy
Netty
Offices
Penny house

Petty
Place of easement
Place of repose
Place of retirement
Reading room
Reredorter
Round the back
Shit-hole
Shooting gallery
Shunkie
Slash house
Spice Islands
Throne room
Thunder box
Tivvy
Waterloo
Windsor Castle

It is said that a former British Foreign Secretary visiting Moscow wanted to impress his hosts and open his speech in Russian. In the heat of the moment, just before he was due to start talking, he forgot how to say Ladies and Gentlemen so hastily sent an aide to go and find the words on the lavatory doors.

Unfortunately the Foreign Secretary started his speech: 'Lavatories and Urinals ...'

Are you sitting comfortably?

A whole lot of holes.

There was a young fellow called Hyde,

Who fell down a privy and died.

His unfortunate brother

Then fell down another

And now they're interred side by side.

A Flush in the Pan

An old lady had a wooden privy seat with a split in the wood. It was extremely uncomfortable every time she sat down on it and she complained bitterly to her landlord who was very slow to do anything about it.

Eventually the landlord sent a joiner round to look at the problem. The man had a long flowing beard and as he leaned on the seat to get a closer look, his weight caused the crack to open. However, when he stood up and released his weight, the split in the seat snapped back together catching his beard.

He tugged and pulled but his beard held firmly in the crack. He pleaded with the old lady to do something, whereupon she went into the house, found a pair of scissors and quickly cut off his beard, leaving a big tuft of hair still in the crack. 'Perhaps you see now', said the old lady, 'how I've suffered for years'.

LOCAL NEWS

'Yesterday thieves broke into the police station and stole the toilets. The police say they have absolutely nothing to go on.'

Thoughts on paper

'Here I sit broken hearted –
Paid a penny and only farted.'

A Flush in the Pan

The story is told of Queen Victoria on a visit to Cambridge being shown round by the Master of Trinity. They paused on a bridge over the river Cam into which untreated sewage flowed.

Her Majesty enquired, 'What are all those pieces of paper floating in the river?'

The Master, without missing a beat, replied, 'Those ma'am, are notices that bathing is forbidden'.

In the great House of Commons,

The core of our land,

When a motion is made,

The member must stand.

In this neat cottage privy,

Now don't on this frown,

When a motion is made,

The member sits down.

A requisition of lavatory paper was known as 'Army Form Blank' and in some Army camps the sergeant-major thought only three pieces of lavatory paper were necessary:

One up, One down, One to polish.

A Flush in the Pan

Welsh farmer living in isolated mid Wales in the 1950s had a holiday cottage which he let out occasionally. A lady from Sussex was going to rent the cottage for the summer but on receiving the details there seemed to be no mention of a lavatory. She wrote anxiously to the farmer asking if there was a WC attached to the cottage.

Being Welsh he thought WC stood for Wesleyan Chapel and wrote her the following letter:

Dear Madam,

The WC is situated some 7 miles from your lodgings in the midst of beautiful scenery and is open Tuesdays, Thursdays, Fridays and Sundays. This is unfortunate if you are in the habit of going frequently, but you will be interested to know that some people take their lunch and make a day of it. Others go by car and arrive just in time.

The accommodation is good and there are about 60 seats but if at anytime you are late arriving, there is plenty of standing room. You will find for your use hymn sheets hanging on the back of the door. I advise you to visit on a Friday as there is an organ recital on that day.

I should be delighted to take you there. My wife and I have not been for 6 months and it pains us very much.

Yours sincerely

May your life be like a new roll of lavatory paper – long and useful.

A Flush in the Pan

A popular name in the Civil Service and the Armed Forces for endless forms and reports was 'bumf' – short for 'bum fodder'.

In days of old when knights were bold,
And paper weren't invented,
They wiped their arse on blades of grass
And walked away contented.

Letter to a Tax Inspector on being informed that a further payment of tax was due:

Dear Sir,

I have your letter in front of me and it will soon be behind me.

There once was an expert on loos,
Who on paper had very strong views,
From the privy he'd come
With print on his bum,
Once again, all behind with the news.

Q: How many men does it take to change an empty loo roll?
A: I'll let you know when it happens.

Someone's got to do it

*The joys of country living with a septic
tank. Some women say they need a man
like a fish needs a bicycle – but when it
comes to rodding out only a man will do.*

o-o-o-o-o-o-o-o-o-o-o-o-o-o-o-o-o-o

A Flush in the Pan

Q: What has four wheels and flies?

A: A nightsoil cart.

Two nightcart men were emptying the privy buckets into their cart when one of the men, Tom Tipler, came back to the almost full cart to find his workmate Mucky Dan leaning over trying to fish something out.

'What are you doing?' asked Tom.

'I put my jacket on the side of the cart and it's fallen in,' said Dan.

'Well for goodness sake,' said Tom, *'it's only an old one, leave it where it is.'*

'I'm not bothered for the jacket,' said Dan, 'but my sandwiches are in the pocket!'

One bucket man, on noticing a smartly dressed lady looking displeased at his presence, was heard to confront her with: 'No use complaining to me lady, this may be shit to you, but it's my bread and butter.'

A Flush in the Pan

A man entered a gents public lavatory and was amazed to find that everything in it was immaculate. The taps gleamed, the mirrors sparkled, the urinals and lavatories were spotless, clean towels were provided, there were several vases of freshly picked flowers and you could see your reflection in the highly polished floor.

The man said to the lavatory attendant, 'You really must be congratulated on the state of this public lavatory. I hope your employers appreciate just how hard you must work to keep it like this.'

The lavatory attendant looked a bit glum. 'Thank you sir, I do my best but you know I have been working here 20 years and have never had a day off.'

'That is disgraceful,' said the man. 'I know the head of your department at the council offices and I shall make a point of speaking to him about this.'

A few weeks later the same man returned to the public lavatory and who should be sitting outside on a deckchair in the sun but the lavatory attendant. He had shorts, sandals and a sunhat on and beside him was a bottle of suncream, a long cool drink and a Jeffrey Archer novel. 'What are you doing?' asked the man.

'I must thank you sir, I am having a lovely time,' said the lavatory attendant. 'That word you had with my boss has done the trick. He said I could have a holiday anytime at my own convenience.'

Songs my mother never sang me

Oh, dear! What can the matter be?

Oh, dear! what can the matter be?

Two old Ladies locked in the lav-a-tory.

They've been there from Mon-day to Sat-ur-day,

No-bod-y knew they were there.

Have you heard about the constipated composer?

He couldn't finish his last movement.

A Flush in the Pan

A popular Girl Guide campfire song reflected the fact that trains at one time discharged the contents of the lavatory onto the railway track. Sung to the tune of Humoresque by Dvorak:

Passengers will please refrain

From passing water when the train

Is standing in the station.

That means YOU!

All porters working underneath

Will get it in the eyes and teeth,

And they don't like it

Any more than you.

So – when the train is in the station,

We encourage constipation.

That has always been

Our golden rule.

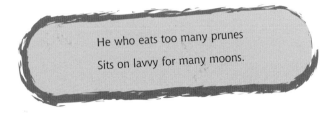

He who eats too many prunes

Sits on lavvy for many moons.

A Flush in the Pan

Who can say if the following is true but the story goes that a church, strapped for cash, applied to the founder of Beecham's Pills, Thomas Beecham (1820-1907), for some new hymn books and found the following verse subtly changed.

Hark! the herald angels sing,

Beecham Pills are just the thing.

Peace on earth and mercy mild,

Two for mother, one for child.

There once was a fair Maid of Kent,

Whose trips to the loos were frequent.

She said as she flushed,

'I will not be rushed,

Nor give up my seat for a gent'.

A Flush in the Pan

Standing room only

n Englishman on a visit to a small town in Wales needed the 'gents' and asked a passing Welshman where he could find a urinal.

The puzzled Welshman replied, 'I'm sorry bach, I know a Huw Jones and a Huw Thomas but I don't know any Huw Rinal. Why don't you ask at the police station round the corner – you can't miss it, it's just next to the gents lavatory.'

A Flush in the Pan

very morning on his way to work a grand lawyer passed an exclusive London club, to which he had been denied membership. Each morning without fail he would go into the club, even though he was not a member, and use the WC. This continued for some time until one morning the hall porter stopped him and said, 'Excuse me sir, do you realise this is a private club?' The lawyer replied in lofty tones, 'Oh is it that as well!'

Q: What do a wedding anniversary and a lavatory bowl have in common?

A: Men always miss them.

ith increasing wealth and prosperity Victorian town councils competed to build the most opulent town halls and public amenities. The council in one northern town held a meeting to debate the necessity and desirability of constructing a magnificent new public urinal.

One ill - educated town councillor, used to cruder terms, refused to vote as he did not understand the word 'urinal'. When it was explained to him, he declared that he would be delighted to vote for the building of a new 'urinal' and not only that – a new 'arsenal' as well.

A Flush in the Pan

+-+-+-+-+-+-+-+-+-+-+-+-+-+-+-+-+-+

> Why do drunk men miss the lavatory?
>
> Why do sober men?

When ordinary British people started taking holidays abroad they were often shocked by the pissoirs of Paris. Here men could urinate in the street, in full view of passers-by, shielded only by a narrow screen at waist height.

A holiday poster advertising a ferry to Europe with the slogan 'Harwich for the Continent' had the famous graffito scrawled underneath: 'And Paris for the Incontinent'.

> Notice in a gentlemen's urinal: 'Please adjust your dress before leaving.'
>
> Written underneath: 'If I could do that, I'd be in the ladies.'

Notice above a gentlemen's urinal; 'If you can aim this high you should join the fire brigade.'

> Seen above a gentlemen's urinal: 'While you're reading this – you're now peeing on your shoes.'

+-+-+-+-+-+-+-+-+-+-+-+-+-+-+-+-+-+

A Flush in the Pan

What goes in must come out

An old farmer had for many years suffered from strong and smelly wind, which was at its worst first thing in the morning. His wife complained bitterly about the strength and loudness of his problem saying, 'One day, Jim, you'll fart so strongly you'll blow your insides out'.

Jim took no notice of her and continued in the same way. One Christmas morning his wife got up early to prepare the turkey. She tiptoed down to the farmhouse kitchen, leaving Jim farting away happily in his sleep. While she was preparing the turkey her hand plunged into the cavity and, as she pulled out the turkey gizzards, she had an idea.

Silently she crept upstairs and without waking Jim, pulled back the waistband of his pyjama bottoms and placed the turkey gizzards inside his pyjamas. She then retired downstairs and waited.

Soon afterwards she heard the most terrible commotion: shouting and screaming, followed by footsteps running along the landing and the bathroom door slamming shut. She thought, 'I'll let him get on with it for a bit.'

Eventually she went upstairs and knocked gently on the bathroom door enquiring sweetly, 'Jim my love, are you all right?'

The farmer flung wide the bathroom door and there he stood, stark naked, the sweat pouring from him in globules, the veins standing out from his puce - coloured face. He gasped, 'Mary, Mary it was just as you said it would be – I have farted my insides out!' 'But,' he went on, 'by the grace of God and these two fingers I've managed to get them back inside again!'

Doctor, doctor, what's good for excessive wind?

Answer: A kite.

How dare you break wind in front of my wife!

I'm sorry, I didn't realise it was her turn.

A Flush in the Pan

A very dignified headmistress went to see her doctor. She explained that she could not stop herself from passing wind and this was proving very difficult when dealing with staff and pupils.

'I really have no control over what's happening,' she said, 'but it is some consolation that when I break wind it neither smells nor makes a noise.' 'Indeed,' she went on, 'since coming into your surgery and talking to you it has happened several times.'

The doctor reached for his pad and wrote out a prescription for her. When the headmistress read it, she asked incredulously, 'Why have you prescribed nasal drops?'

'Well,' said the doctor, 'first we'll sort out your nose and then we'll have a go at your hearing.'

From a 15th century Boke of Curtasye:

'Beware of thy hinder parts from gunblasting.'

You may be high and mighty

Or folk of humble part,

When seated on the lavvy

A fart is still a fart.

A Flush in the Pan

Q: What do you call it when you sit on your glasses?

A: Flatulens.

Q: Why do men break wind more than women?

A: Because women won't shut up long enough to build up the required pressure.

On breaking wind:

Better an empty house than a bad tenant.

A Flush in the Pan

A fart is a breeze

It gives the belly ease.

It warms up the bedclothes

And kills off the fleas.

Diarrhoea waits for no man.

◦-◦-◦-◦-◦-◦-◦-◦-◦-◦-◦-◦-◦-◦-◦-◦-◦

The Slow Movement

During the First World War, Beecham's Pills sent lavatory paper to the troops with the following advice printed on: 'Take Beecham's Pills for active service.'

Have you heard about the constipated accountant?

He couldn't budget.

In springtime, mothers gave an extra special strong dose of purgative to the family to clear out and pep up the system after the long winter months.

Mrs Keenlyside's Spring Medicine

Into a large jug place:

12 senna pods

2 teaspoons of Epsom Salts

Juice of a lemon

1 flat teaspoon of cream of tartar

Sugar to taste

Infuse the above in about 3 pints of boiling water, which has cooled slightly. Drink plenty and stand back for action.

◦-◦-◦-◦-◦-◦-◦-◦-◦-◦-◦-◦-◦-◦-◦-◦-◦

A Flush in the Pan

 ld Frank had been constipated for a week so he went along to the local chemist to ask for something to relieve the problem.

The chemist said he had just what he needed but it had to be measured carefully and he must ask him some questions first. So, taking a large jar of white powder off the shelf, the chemist asked Frank, 'How far is your lavatory from your cottage?'

'About 35 yards,' replied Frank. So the chemist put some powder in the container.

'Have you got a bolt on your back door?' asked the chemist. Frank replied that he had and so the chemist shook more powder into the container.

'How many steps up your stairs?'

'I think about 10 or 11, I don't rightly know,' said Frank. The chemist poured some more powder in the container.

'Do you wear a belt or braces on your trousers?' enquired the chemist.

'Both,' replied Frank and with that the chemist shook even more powder out and handed Frank the container.

'There you are, that'll see you all right. A shilling please. But remember the moment you feel the urge you must go at once.'

A few days later the chemist met Frank in the street and enquired, 'How are you, did my powder work?'

'Oh ah,' said Frank, *'I should say it worked all right – but you beat me by 3 yards!'*

Wit and wisdom

Francois Rabelais (c1495-1553), French author and monk, listed the many items that could be used for bottom wiping but declared, 'I maintain that of all the torcheculs, arsewips, bumfodders, tailnapkins, bunghole cleansers and wipe-breeches, there is none in the world comparable to the neck of a goose.'

Notice in pub lavatory: 'Don't throw your cigarette ends in the lavatory – it makes them impossible to light.'

The 4th Earl of Chesterfield (1694-1773) in a series of letters over 30 years to his natural son Philip Stanhope gave him much anxious fatherly advice. A letter in 1747, written while his son was travelling on the Continent, advised him to manage his time well and recommended the actions of a gentleman he had once known.

'Who was so good a manager of his time, that he would not even lose that small portion of it which the call of nature obliged him to pass in the necessary-house; but gradually went through all the Latin poets, in those moments. He bought, for example, a common edition of Horace, of which

A Flush in the Pan

❍═❍═❍═❍═❍═❍═❍═❍═❍═❍═❍═❍═❍═❍═❍═❍

he tore off gradually a couple of pages, carried them with him to that necessary place, read them first, and then sent them down as a sacrifice to Cloacina. Thus was so much time fairly gained; and I recommend you to follow his example. It is better than only doing what you cannot help doing at those moments; and it will make any book which you shall read in that manner, very present to your mind.'

A dvice from Dr Samuel Johnson (1709-84), the great English lexicographer, against the fashion for quilted padded lavatory seats. 'No Sir, the plain board is the best.'

> Notice in pub lavatory: 'Don't throw your cigarette ends in the urinal – we don't piss in your ashtrays.'

T he Duke of Wellington (1769-1852), when asked by a gentleman if he could give him the piece of advice that had been the most useful on his many campaigns, replied, 'Certainly, sir; never lose an opportunity to pump-ship.'

❍═❍═❍═❍═❍═❍═❍═❍═❍═❍═❍═❍═❍═❍═❍═❍

A Flush in the Pan

Lord Baden-Powell (1857-1941), in more innocent times, wrote *Scouting for Boys* in 1908. He believed strongly in regularity and having a 'rear' every day and if there was any difficulty he advised: 'drink plenty of water ... and practise body-twisting exercises.'

The great WC

When Sir Winston Churchill (1874-1965) was Leader of the Opposition, the Lord Privy Seal was said to have insulted him in the House of Commons. He returned home highly incensed, followed shortly by the Lord Privy Seal who had been instructed to apologise to Churchill by the Leader of the House of Commons.

Winston Churchill's butler answered the door and asked the Lord Privy Seal to wait as his master was otherwise engaged. In fact he was on the lavatory.

The butler knocked on the bathroom door and advised Winston Churchill that the Lord Privy Seal was here to see him.

Whereupon Churchill growled, 'Tell the Lord Privy Seal that I am sealed to my privy and I can only deal with one shit at a time!'

On seeing his portrait by Graham Sutherland it was said that Winston Churchill commented that it made him look as if he were straining a stool.

Odd Flushings

If you want a wet surprise – pull the chain before you rise.

**Ancient wisdom –
a swinging chain means a warm seat.**

A Flush in the Pan

⚙⚙⚙⚙⚙⚙⚙⚙⚙⚙⚙⚙⚙⚙⚙⚙⚙⚙

An old lady living alone during the Second World War was sitting in her WC down the bottom of the garden when an air raid started and a bomb dropped on her house. The noise, debris and dust were horrendous. When the fire brigade arrived they found the house flattened but the WC still standing. Wrenching open the door they came across the old lady sitting there, dazed and confused. Tearfully she explained, 'All I did was pull the chain'.

Overheard in an antiques shop:

Antique dealer: 'This chair is very old – it's Queen Anne.'

Customer: 'Oh yes, how can you tell?'

Antique dealer: 'The letters QA are carved underneath – that stands for Queen Anne.'

Customer: 'If that stands for Queen Anne, I've got a door back home that dates back to William the Conqueror.'

⚙⚙⚙⚙⚙⚙⚙⚙⚙⚙⚙⚙⚙⚙⚙⚙⚙⚙

A man was staying in lodgings and there was no indoor lavatory, only a WC down a very long garden. Going to use it for the first time he was disconcerted on coming out to see a little old man in a flat cap and a long mackintosh standing in front of the WC glaring at him.

'Have you just been in there?' demanded the little old man.

'*Yes,*' answered the man.

'And did you use it?' asked the little old man.

'*Yes,*' answered the man.

'And did you see that piece of string in there?' said the little old man.

'*Yes.*'

'And did you pull it?'

'*Yes.*'

'I thought so,' raged the little old man. 'You've just let all my bloody pigeons out!'

What was it, my darling, you emptied on me?

I came back again at a quarter to four

Whoops! Splash! You've done it once more!

(*From 'Herefordshire Privies' by Paddy Ariss*)

A Flush in the Pan

A n old couple had for years made do with an old bucket privy in the garden. The local council decided to award them a grant to put a flush WC just outside the back door. They were very excited when it was finished and the old gentleman kindly said his wife could go first and use the new lavatory.

So the old lady went in but failed to reappear and after half an hour her husband began to worry. He banged on the door shouting, 'Are you all right in there?'

His wife replied in an anxious little voice, 'Well. I don't know dear, every time I get hold of the chain to pull myself up there's a rush of water goes right through me.'

Why is that boy hiding under the bed?

Because he thinks he's a little potty.

Chamber Music

In earlier times, chamberpots were often given as wedding presents.

'This pot it is a present sent.

Some mirth to make is only meant.

We hope the same you'll not refuse,

But keep it safe and oft to use.

When in it you want to piss,

Remember them who sent you this.'

Many were the rhymes that adorned the chamber pots of old, among them:

Keep me clean and use me well

And what I see I'll never tell

A Flush in the Pan

N otice on the bedroom wall of an upmarket boarding house in the days when salesmen were called 'commercial travellers' and there were only outside lavatories:

'Would any gentleman using the chamberpot during the night please cover the contents with a newspaper as the steam from the chamberpot rusts the bedsprings.'

A chamberpot by any other name:

Gazunder	Potty
Jerry	Rogue-with-one-ear
Pisspot	Tea voider
Po	Thundermug

'Oh, I see you still keep a jerry under the bed.'

'Oh no, it's a carpet vase.'

The Writing on the Wall

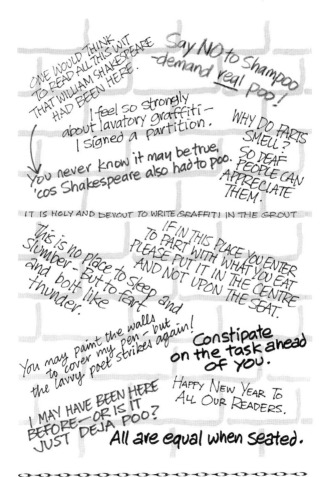

ONE WOULD THINK TO READ ALL THIS WIT THAT WILLIAM SHAKESPEARE HAD BEEN HERE.

Say NO to Shampoo – demand real poo!

I feel so strongly about lavatory graffiti – I signed a partition.

WHY DO FARTS SMELL? SO DEAF PEOPLE CAN APPRECIATE THEM.

You never know it may be true, 'cos Shakespeare also had to poo.

IT IS HOLY AND DEVOUT TO WRITE GRAFFITI IN THE GROUT

This is no place to slumber – But to sleep and and bolt like thunder.

IF IN THIS PLACE YOU ENTER TO PART WITH WHAT YOU EAT PLEASE PUT IT IN THE CENTRE AND NOT UPON THE SEAT.

You may paint the walls to cover my pen – but the lavvy poet strikes again!

Constipate on the task ahead of you.

I MAY HAVE BEEN HERE BEFORE – OR IS IT JUST DEJA POO?

HAPPY NEW YEAR TO ALL OUR READERS.

All are equal when seated.

A Flush in the Pan

○◇○◇○◇○◇○◇○◇○◇○◇○◇○◇○◇○◇○

Some people cannot resist writing on lavatory walls. Even in first century Herculaneum the ash from the eruption of Vesuvius in AD 79 preserved this example: APOLLONIVS MEDICVS TITI IMP. HIC CACARIT BENE.

Translated as 'Apollonius physician of Emperor Titus had a good evacuation of the bowels here.'

> If you think the bottom's dropped out of your world,
>
> Drink ... (insert the beer of your choice),
>
> And the world will drop out of your bottom.

Graffiti found on the walls of the gentlemen's lavatory in the Inns of Court:

I do not like this place at all,

The seat is too high and the hole is too small.

And written underneath:

You leave yourself open to the obvious retort,

Your bottom's too big and your legs are too short.

○◇○◇○◇○◇○◇○◇○◇○◇○◇○◇○◇○◇○

Seen on the wall of a theatre lavatory:

LADIES – Please remain seated during the entire performance.

A Flush in the Pan